Comforter
001

Dog
002

Turnspit
003

Dalmatian or Coach Dog
004

Springer or Cocker
005

Mastiff
006

Old English Hound
007

Irish Greyhound
008

Newfoundland Dog
009

010

012

Greenland Dog
011

Beagle
014

Large Water-Spaniel
013

Small Water-Spaniel
015

016

Large Rough Water Dog
017

Harrier
018

Greyhound
019

Spanish Pointer
020

Cur Dog
021

Fox Hound
022

023

Shepherd's Dog
024

Ban-Dog
025

Terrier
026

English Setter
027

Bull-Dog
028

029

030

031

032

033

034

035

036

037

038

039

040

041

Hunter
042

043

Improved Cart-Horse
044

Common Cart-Horse
045

Race Horse
046

047

048

Arabian Horse
049

Black Horse
050

051

052

053

054

055

Old English Road-Horse
056

Mule
057

Ass
058

059

060

Arabian Camel
061

Bactrian Camel
062

Cameleopard
063

Zebra
064

065

066

Wild Cattle
067

068

Holstein or Dutch Breed
069

Long-Horned or Lancaster Breed
070

Improved Holstein or Dutch Breed
071

Improved Holstein or Dutch Breed
072

Wild Cattle
073

074

075

076

Zebu
077

078

Buffalo
079

Musk-Bull
080

Lancashire Ox
081

Urus or Wild Bull
082

Bison
083

084

085

Wallachian Sheep
086

Heath Ram of Improved Breed
087

Wedder of Mr. Culley's Breed
088

Many-Horned Sheep
089

Tees-Water Improved Breed
090

Cheviot Ram
091

Tees-Water Old or Unimproved Breed
092

Leicestershire Improved Breed
093

094

Tartarian Sheep
095

Dunky or Dwarf Sheep
096

097

098

Chamois Goat
099

Black-Faced or Heath Ram
100

Goat of Angora
101

Syrian Goat
102

Pied Goat
103

Wood-Goat
104

Ibex
105

Common Goat
106

Ibex
107

Mouflon or Musmon
108

African Wild Boar or Wood Swine
109

Peccary or Mexican Hog
110

111

Wild Boar
112

Babiroussa
113

114

Chinese Kind
115

Common Boar
116

Sow of Improved Breed
117

Jackal
118

Arctic Fox
119

120

Fox
121

Striped Hyena
122

Racoon
123

Greyhound Fox
124

Spotted Hyena
125

New South Wales Wolf
126

Wolf
127

Stag or Red-Deer
128

Elk-Antelope
129

130

Fallow-Deer
131

Gnu
132

Chevrotain and Meminna
133

134

135

Springer
136

Axis or Ganges Stag
137

138

Elk
140

Rein-Deer
139

141

Common Antelope
142

Roe-Buck
143

Musk
144

145

146

147

148

149

150

Margay or Tiger Cat
151

Ocelot
152

Cougar
153

Leopard
154

155

Lynx
156

157

Jaguar
158

Black Tiger
159

Serval
160

Tiger
161

162

Panther
163

Elephant
164

165

Elephant
166

Two-Horned Rhinoceros
167

Long-Nosed Tapir
168

Hippopotamus
169

Rhinoceros
170

Walrus or Sea Horse
171

Ursine Seal or Sea-Bear
172

Mongooz
173

Baboon
174

Barbary Ape
175

Ring-Tailed Macauco
176

Striated Monkey
177

Dog-Faced Baboon
178

Green Monkey
179

Ribbed-Nose Baboon
180

Red-Tailed Monkey
181

20   PRIMATES

Long-Armed Ape
182

183

Varied Monkey or Mona
184

185

186

187

188

Bear
189

190

Polar or Great White Bear
191

192

Hare
193

Rabbit
194

195

Grey Squirrel
198

Domestic Rabbit
196

197

199

Long-Tailed Squirrel
200

Squirrel
201

Flying Squirrel
202

Barbary Squirrel
203

Water Rat
204

205

Quebec Marmot
206

Mouse
207

Marmot
208

Lapland Marmot
209

Musk-Rat of Canada
210

Long-Tailed Field Mouse
211

Rat
212

Lesser Dormouse or Garden Squirrel
213

Short-Tailed Field Mouse
214

Dwarf Mouse
215

Tailless Marmot
216

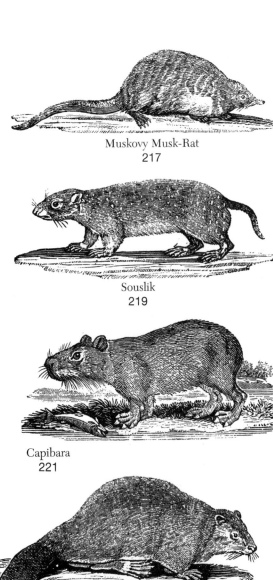

Muskovy Musk-Rat
217

Hamster
218

Souslik
219

Dormouse or Ground Squirrel
220

Capibara
221

Guinea-Pig or Restless Cavy
222

Beaver
223

Monax
224

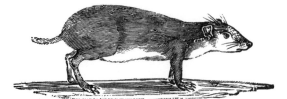

Akouchi
226

Spotted Cavy
225

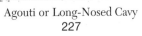

Agouti or Long-Nosed Cavy
227

Jerboa
228

Fourmart
229

Stoat
230

Ferret
231

Pine-Weasel or Yellow-Breasted Martin
232

Sable
233

Ichneumon
234

Weasel
235

Fossane
236

Badger
237

Wolverine or Glutton
238

Ratel
239

Skunk
240

Coati or Brazilian Weasel
241

Suricate or Four-Toed Weasel
242

Zibet
243

Genet
244

Civet
245

Water Shrew Mouse
246

Shrew Mouse
247

Tendrac
248

Tanrec
249

Ant-Eater
250

Great Manis
251

Nine-Banded Armadillo
252

Sloth
253

Six-Banded Armadillo
254

Kabassou
255

Brazilian Porcupine
257

Porcupine
256

Hedge-Hog or Urchin
258

Canada Porcupine
259

Platypus
260

SLOTHS, ANTEATERS, ARMADILLOS, PORCUPINES, HEDGEHOGS AND PLATYPUSES   27

Spotted Opossum of New South Wales
261

Phalanger
262

Opossum of Van Diemen's Land
263

Kangaroo Rat of
New South Wales
264

Kangaroo
265

Wombach
266

Flying Opossum
of New South Wales
267

Saragoy   268   Murine

Squirrel Opossum
269

Mexican Opossum
270

Short-Eared Bat
271

Ternate Bat
272

Long-Eared Bat
273

Frog
274

Turtle
275

Brazilian Chameleon
276

277

278

279

280

281

282

283

285

284

287

286

289

288

291

290

293

292

294

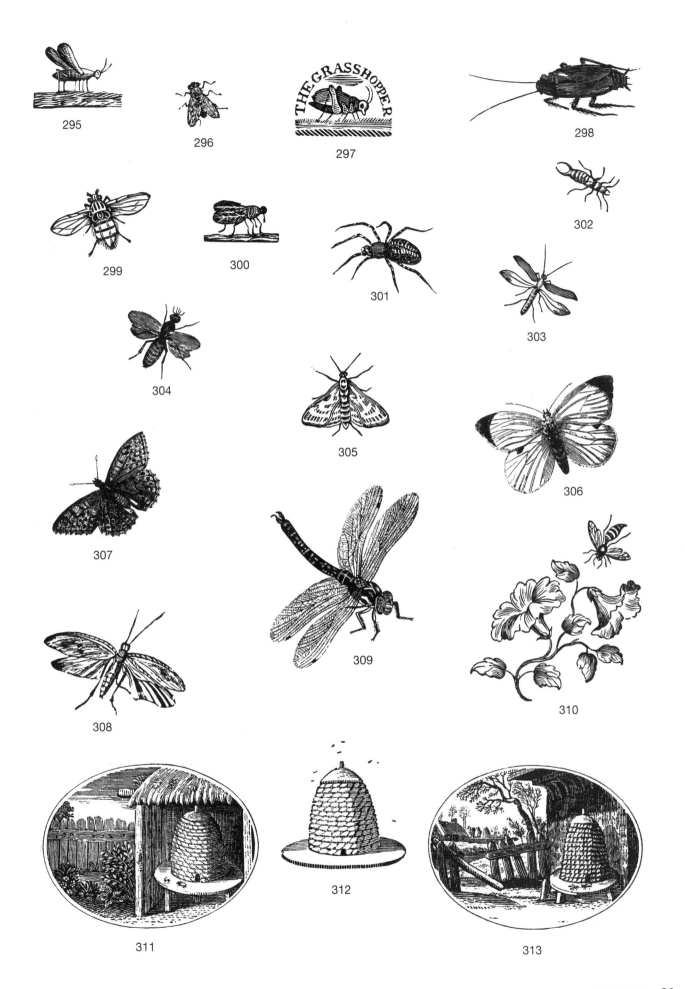

295

296

THE GRASSHOPPER

297

298

299

300

301

302

303

304

305

306

307

308

309

310

311

312

313

Swift
314

Redstart
315

Nuthatch
316

Hedge Warbler
317

Grasshopper Warbler
318

Goldfinch
319

Grey Wagtail
320

Mountain Linnet
321

Sparrow
322

Bullfinch
323

Grosbeak
324

Mountain Finch
325

Wren
326

Cross-Bill
327

Redbreast
328

Black-Headed Bunting
329

Yellow Bunting
330

Coal Titmouse
331

Titmouse
332

Stonechat
333

Ring Dove
334

Woodlark
335

Turtle Dove
336

Wild Pigeon
337

Rook
338

Nutcracker
339

Starling
340

Jay
341

Silky Starling
342

Raven
343

Blackbird
344

Yellow Owl
345

Snowy Owl
346

Little Owl
347

Female Short-Eared Owl
348

Eagle Owl
349

Short-Eared Owl
350

Tawny Owl
351

352

Ring Paroquet
353

Peacock
354

Little Guinea Paroquet
355

Golden Winged Paroquet
356

Sapphire Crowned Paroquet
357

Night-Jar
358

Hoopoe
359

Kingfisher
360

Barred Woodpecker
361

Kingfisher
362

Pied Woodpecker
363

Green Woodpecker
364

Wryneck
365

Three-Toed Woodpecker
366

Female Kestrel
367

Bearded Vulture
368

Peregrine Falcon
369

Crested Vulture
370

Secretary
371

372

373

Buzzard
374

Little Black and
Orange Coloured
Indian Hawk
375

Hen-Harrier
376

377

Honey Buzzard
378

Osprey
379

Golden Eagle
380

Muskovy Duck
381

Mallard
382

Common Duck
383

384

Shoveler
385

Goosander
386

387

Goose
388

389

390

Pheasant
391

Wood Grouse
392

393

Cock
394

Partridge
395

Quail
396

Turkey
397

Domestic Cock
398

Green Sandpiper
399

Turnstone
400

Sanderling
401

Golden Plover
402

Dotterel
403

Dunlin
404

Curlew
405

Ruff
406

Glossy Ibis
407

Heron
408

Long-Legged Plover
409

Stork
410

411

Spoonbill
412

Crane
413

Razor-Bill
414

Tippet Grebe
415

Dusky Grebe
416

Little Auk
417

Great-Crested Grebe
418

Great Auk
419

Puffin
420

Black-Backed Gull
421

Lesser Tern
422

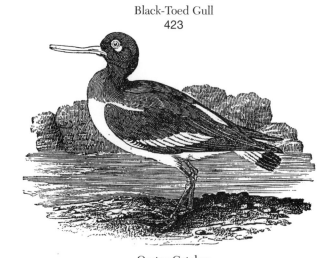

Black-Toed Gull
423

Crested Cormorant
424

Oyster-Catcher
425

Wagel (Gull)
426

Avoset
427

INDEX TO THE ANIMALS